in a
house
by the sea

in a
house
by the sea

sandy gingras

DOWN
THE
SHORE
PUBLISHING
Harvey Cedars, NJ

Down The Shore Publishing Corp.
Box 3100, Harvey Cedars, NJ 08008

www.down-the-shore.com

The words "Down The Shore" and the Down The Shore Publishing logo
are a registered U.S. Trademark.

Printed in China
2 4 6 8 10 9 7 5 3 1
First Printing

Library of Congress Cataloging-in-Publication Data

Gingras, Sandy, 1958-
In a house by the sea/Sandy Gingras.
p. cm.
ISBN 1-59322-013-8
1. Seaside resorts--Literary collections. 2. Vacation homes--Literary
collections. 3.
Beaches--Literary collections. I. Title.

PS3607.I45815 2005
818'.609--dc22

2005041408

contents

what this book
is about

When my publisher asked me to tell him what this book was about, I paused. This is always a moment in a writer's life. "What AM I doing?" I asked myself. "Well," I said, "it's, you know, a little bit of this, a little bit of that..." My publisher is very polite. He cocked his head inquiringly and smiled. "It's like a mish-mash of ideas and doodles," I started again, "Dribs and drabs." It was starting to sound like a nursery rhyme. "I have IDEAS," I said more insistently, "about being a woman, and being a woman at the beach." I was gathering steam, "I did some little watercolors. I wrote some essays that are all different, but connected somehow. The book is kind of like me...kind of like my life...you know?" I said with a flourish of my arm. A grand sweeping gesture. "I'm sorry," I said picking up the pages I had knocked to the ground.

We were sitting in the back "yard" of a tangled vine-y ruin of a building over 200 years old that my publisher had just bought as a restoration project. We were perched on some ratty plastic folding chairs that were pulled up to a white iron wobbly table. In piles around us, there was an old refrigerator, a push lawn mower, an antique tea cup, a rubber ball, a plastic rocking horse, and a stack of old green shutters. My publisher had a smudge of dirt on his cheek, a cobweb on his ear. He had spent the morning going through boxes of receipts from the general store that was once here. "I guess it's not really together enough to be a book," I apologized, "it really is just a conglomeration of odd tidbits, the inside of my brain and my heart." My publisher looked at me happily. He nodded. He looked around at the rubble and the treasures around us, the rusted pipes, the weathered boards, a child's high chair painted pink, the weeds and the old climbing roses, the dappled shade and sunlight in the plastic aqua pool. We were in the midst of the detritus and trappings of a life, all the flourishings and dead ends, the foolish moments and the triumphs, the dribs and the drabs of it all. "It sounds great," he said.

at the crossroads
of Life

this is what makes me

It's the first day of summer. I'm ten or maybe twelve. School's out, and the world is stretching itself into one long basking day after another. My father is driving my family to the beach in our station wagon, his one arm (tan from the bicep down) angles out the window and he's drumming his fingers on the car door. "Up, Up and Away" is playing on the scratchy car radio. I'm sitting on my one folded leg to get a little height so I can be the first one to see the ocean as we go over the bridge. I'm trying

suddenLy sand on The side of the road

not to throw up from too much excitement and too much time in the back seat. We're getting there. The air begins to smell like salt. There's suddenly sand on the side of the road.

When we pull into the overgrown driveway of our summer house, it's noon. It's high noon. It's the heart of the day. I run over the dune. The sky is huge. The water is blue and glistening and utterly calm. The tide is lower than it's ever been. Come to me, it is calling. The sand is an endless stretch of beckoning flatness.

it's the heart of the day

Run on me, it is saying. A little sailboat is making its slow way along the horizon. I'm half girl, half woman, just like I'll always be. I realize suddenly that summer is a verb. Beach is a verb. I am a verb. I want to beach, beach, beach, summer, summer, summer, I, I, I. Do you know that moment? Do you know what it's like when there's enough life to grasp and squeeze and you can feel the juice running down your arms. When there's enough life to waste and sift through your fingers and squander on pure silliness. When there's that much abundance. That much possibility...

up, up and away

You do. I know you do. If only in your imagination. And that's all you really need. Because this moment never really happened to me either. A couple parts maybe, but the rest is a mixture of fiction and dream and desire. Yet it defines me more than any "real" memory. However I grow, my mind is anchored in this moment. And wherever I go, my heart steers toward it as sure as a compass. It's not nostalgia. And it's not stuckness. It's just an idea I have inside me: A beach (more emotional that geographic) that I keep walking on. A summer (more attitude than season) that I keep longing for. This is what moves me. This is what makes me a beach woman.

I am a verb

A is for Attitude

A is for Away. Away, beach woman, away with you to the beach! You've had enough reality.

B is for the Book you can finally read without interruption.

C is for Coconut suntan lotion. C is also for Cabana Boy... as in, "Cabana Boy, can you put this coconut suntan lotion on my back."

D is for Dinner out. Again? Mais Oui!

E is for Entirely immobilized.

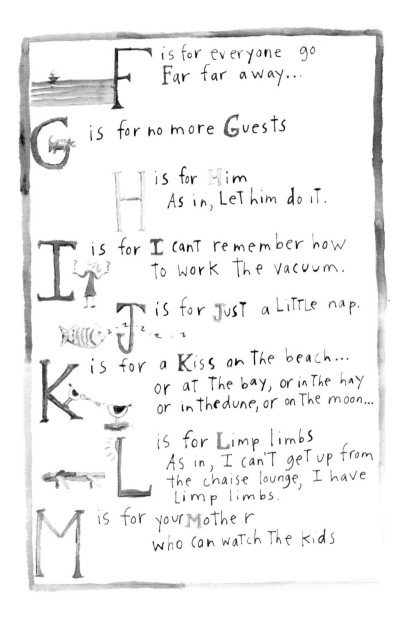

F is for everyone go
Far far away...

G is for no more Guests

H is for Him
   As in, Let him do it.

I is for I can't remember how
   to work the vacuum.

J is for Just a little nap.

K is for a Kiss on the beach...
   or at the bay, or in the hay
   or in the dune, or on the moon...

L is for Limp limbs
   As in, I can't get up from
   the chaise lounge, I have
   Limp limbs.

M is for your Mother
   who can watch the kids

N is for the blond streaks in your hair (which occur Naturally).

O is for O goody you cooked dinner.

P is for Pina Colada with a slice of pineapple and a cherry and a happy little paper umbrella in it.

Q is for absolute peace and Quiet.

R is for a beach chair fully Reclined.

S is for a Superficial magazine and how sufficient that can be.

Very active woman

T is for The Time you painted my Toenails ("Totally Twisted Crimson"). Your big hands on that little brush...aah!

U is for Utilizing the hammock.

V is for understanding (at last) that Very imperfect can be very lovely.

W is for Well, well, you haven't aged a bit.

X is for eXtra glamorous sunglasses.

Y is for yes, I will have another Pina Colada.

Z is for zither and Zoology and Zena the Warrior Princess and all those things that you will never do or be, and how perfectly ok that is with you.

moods

in here somewhere,
see if you can
find me

won't open up

shining

stepped on

wound tight

brainy

hooked
on
you

like a rock

practically perfect
in every way

needs a good
wine sauce

crabby

paralyzed

danger danger

do I look fat

a beach house:
what the realtor should
have told you

Let it have the feel and smell of the beach in it. Let the salt and the sand buff the boards, let the colors bleach. Let the shells collect, let the wind blow, let the towels flap on the line. Easy does it... Let the hard stuff soften. Let the harsh things fade. Let it have the soul of the beach in it. Do you know what I mean? It doesn't matter what it cost or how big it is or what couch you put where. Simplicity is not for sale. Neither is peace. You have to live it. I'm sorry but you do. The realtor should have told you this.

You have to love in this house. You have to remember yourself here. You have to go out onto your decks, sit on them and breathe. In these rooms, you have to live. You have to laugh here. And kiss and tickle and play, nap and yawn and read, bask and dream. Allow all the good verbs. Let them romp. And your kids have to learn how to swim here, manage a rip tide, cut their feet on shells, sink a little into the marsh, have their first crush on a lifeguard, their first kiss in the dunes. They have to burn and dive, they have to be tossed by waves, they have to soar their kites far over your heads. You know they do...

Don't plan the day. It's OK, it's OK. Really it is. If there's sand on your feet... If the chairs don't match...If nothing gets done... Can you let it be? Can you feel how right it is?

Let there be pencil lines on the white kitchen paneling where the kids' heights get marked every summer. Let the bikes rust. Let the bayberry bush grow wild and unruly in the front yard (it gives the porch that green shady shimmery scent and makes it feel like such a secret place). Let the freezer have a plastic bag of minnows sitting on the shelf next to the carton of ice cream. Let the plates be paper. Let the tomato plant grow out of the compost pile. Let there be stories in this room. A mess made there. Rest in that chair. Close your eyes. Let it be what it is.

The decorator should have told you. The realtor should have told you. A beach house doesn't come furnished with life. It doesn't have simplicity built in. You can't buy the mood. Even if you have a lot of money. You have to live it in.

flip-flop moods

Who invented the flip-flop? Such a strange and sassy creation. So much personality in its snap. So much flip in its flop. So utilitarian. So simple. And yet the complexities, the variations, the choices! So unisex and yet so flirtatious. I am not a shoe woman. But I do have my fair feminine share of flip-flops. I may unconsciously slip on a pair each summer morning, but somehow they perfectly match (if not the rest of my clothes) my mood. When I look down, I know exactly where I stand....

don't flip flop on that!

dog-chewed,
went-in-bay,
sunk-in-mud,
worn-thin,
no-color-left...
face it: I can't
let go

feeling a Little
fishy

buoyant (more
Like little pontoon
boats than shoes) for
deep days so I can
float through

I wish I was
in Hawaii...
I wish I was
in Hawaii...

neon weird textured
plastic (curly astro-
turf?) because there's
a Little Wal-Mart
in all of us

I can
still
fit
in
these

I am a
lanky
Looming
runway
model
(I can so walk
in these)

call me
Ivana

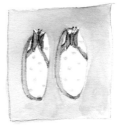

transforming
into something
better...

isn't it still
the age of
aquarius?

hormonally
beachy
(teeth are larger
than they appear
in image)

25

what the beach house is for...

The beach house is where the suitcase gets unpacked
and the groceries get put away
and where, if the office calls, your father is not home.
The beach house is for your father to breathe easy
and for your mother to wear her sun dress.
The windows are for letting the sky in
and the salty smell too.
The curtains are for blowing like ghosts at night.
The screens are to hold the dampness in little squares
and where the flies bang their heads trying to get in.
The roof is for rain to click and tap its song on.
The porch is for smelling storms before they get here —
electric and marshy and yellowy gray
and for your mother to say come inside now
when the lightning starts.
The screen door is for going outside
to see how huge the harvest moon is.
The stairs are to creak
if you try to sneak down them
when your parents are dancing their fancy dance class dance
to the Frank Sinatra music in the living room.
The stairs are for making spooky noises on their own at night
and for the dog to click her nails on.
The porch is to sit on and tell stories
and to swing on idly and make creaky porch swing noises.

and for when your grandmother visits
and she wants to sit next to your grandfather and smile
and pat his hand.
The porch is for letting roses climb on
and for playing Parcheesi at night
and for moths to come thrumming around the light.

The beach house is for a big old stove in the kitchen
where you can boil the crabs
and a kitchen table you can crack them on.
The kitchen is to make pot and pan noises
and for morning sunlight to come in

and make a square that the cat can lie in
and to make the whole house smell like coffee
when you wake up.
The kitchen table is for Scrabble
and the kitchen notepad is to write the score
and what your mother should buy in the market
tomorrow.

The beach house bedroom is to whisper in
and to put your grandmother's quilt in
and to see the stars out the window
It's where you put your fairy wand,
your pirate hat, and all your secret magical stuff.
The closet is for your flip-flops.
The pull out couch is where we put Uncle Jimmy.
The upstairs hall is to put the little basketball net
 so the boys can play basketball on rainy days
and also to practice your putting,
and where your mother says that all the
fingerprints
like to go.

The big chair is for reading mysteries.
The carpet is for tiddly winks
and for the dog to lie down OOF
in the middle of everyone the way she likes to
when there are people visiting.
The living room is for making a fire in the fireplace
and toasting marshmallows on big forks
and for practicing the piano.
The rocking chair is for learning how to crochet.

The couch is to daydream on
and for M & M's and pennies and pen caps
and sand to hide between the cushions.
The TV is for mom to say turn that thing off
and go outside and play.

The yard is for birds to come in and sing
and for the flag to go up
and snap in the wind.
The yard is where the good shells end up,
even the ones that were supposed to be in that craft project.
The yard is for welcoming
and for the mailbox so Timmy the mailman stops to talk,
and to park the bike in.
The shed is for crab traps and fishing poles
and the oars for the row boat.
The shed is to clean because nobody hangs things
on their little hooks.
The garden is to grow too many tomatoes in
and for the zinnias to bloom so magically
that your father says he thinks he must be doing something right.
The butterfly bush is where the butterflies really like to land
all summer long.

The beach house is for closing the door during the winter,
and for leaving the quiet
on the shelves with the old Nancy Drew mysteries
and the Monopoly game and the big conch shell DJ found
and the driftwood that the dog chewed a little bit.
The beach house is for coming back to.
It's for opening up again.

how to build a castle

Just start somewhere.

Who can leave the world untouched?.

Use your hands so you can feel it.

Use what washes up so that the castle grows from what is already here.

The kids who join you (and they will...as soon as you begin) will help you and will find things that you never could have found.

They will name the castles "The Crab Shell Hotel" " The Crooked Palace of Sand," "The Road of Broken Shells," and "The Pool of Dreamy Dreams" so that you'll become attached to these places. Within an hour, it will be a world and you will be in love with it.

And you will know all of the childrens' names.

Wipe the sand from that one's eye.

Everyone needs a buried treasure: Put an X somewhere.

Everyone needs a high tower where the beautiful princess is imprisoned: Make little crumbling steps with your finger that she cannot climb down

Everyone needs a road that goes nowhere.

Everyone needs a labyrinth to be lost in.

Smooth it all with your palm.

Build a dragon who might guard the city? Eat the city? Turn into a prince and marry the princess?

It's all possible.

Get sunburned shoulders. Get sand in your bathing suit.

Race against the tide. Because the tide will be coming in...it always is when you build a castle.

So build a wall and a moat and then another wall.

These are hopeless tasks, but build them anyway...
You know you have to.
Put your whole being into them and then laugh when they crumble.
Go ahead, laugh.
This is your world...
Get down on your knees in the Crooked Palace of Sand.
Immerse yourself in the Pool of Dreamy Dreams.
Fly the flag of seaweed.
These are your unclimbable steps,
This is your buried treasure.
Love your dragon prince with all your dragon heart.
And when you have lost to the tide, join in the losing.
Jump your feet all over your towers.
Then splash into the waves with all the other
denizens of the lost world:
The lost boys and the lost girls.
Dive and float and spew little fountains of water.
We lose worlds like this all the time.
The world is sand
The world is fluid
Build with it.

beach woman
bLown away

these are a few
(well, a hundred)
of my favorite summer
beach things

*"When the dog bites, when the bee stings, when I'm feeling sad, I simply
remember my favorite things and then I don't feel so bad..."
(From The Sound of Music)*

*"When you're worried and you can't sleep, count your blessings instead
of sheep. And you'll fall asleep counting your blessings..."
(From White Christmas)*

I don't understand how certain phenomena come about. How we get into the habit
of only thinking a certain way? Take lists, for example. I only make "To Do" lists. Or
sometimes I make "I want" lists (like at Christmas) or "I need" lists (like before I go to
the Acme market). But all my lists are about the future and what I don't have. Think, if
I woke up in the morning and made a list of what I already have, how bountiful my life
would feel. And what if I started doing that old fashioned prayer-like thing of counting
my blessings before I went to sleep at night. Wouldn't I feel more restful?

All I had to do was to begin a list like this to realize how full my life is. I could go on and
on. Lists like this are spiritual. They are litanies of peace and thankfulness and happiness.
And they are contagious (you can't stop!). When
it's summertime at the beach, a list like this is easy.
There is beauty all around us; we don't have to buy
it, all we have to do it notice it.

1. The little scoops of shade in sandy footprints
2. Salt shakers that have rice inside of them to
absorb the dampness
3. "Come on Baby, Light my Fire" playing on
a scratchy radio at the beach–all the yearny

dangerous hopefulness of love

4. The Good Humor man

5. Barbecued hotdogs with sweet mustard and relish

6. Diving under a wave

7. Pisser clams

8. Halter tops

9. The moon lighting up the whole beach

10. So many people visiting that you have to have an adult table and a kids' table

11. Ghost crabs

12. Belly laughs

13. The shapes of clouds

14. A crooked dock, the board that creaks, the uneven board where you have to watch your step, the dried bait pressed into the gray boards, the lappy echoey sound of the water underneath

15. The huge folded patience of an egret

16. How your husband looks in a bathing suit and his reading glasses

17. Cotton candy (pink)

18. Sitting in Morrison's Restaurant watching the boats go by

19. The electric fried food asphalty smell of the town when the evening is just beginning

20. Floating docks

21. All the little compartments of a tackle box and how it unfolds like an accordion

22. Melon balls

23. Taper candles

24. The day that the tide gets so low you can see the rusty remnants of the barge that sank in the storm of '62

25. The sweepy exhilarating blast of the lifeguard whistle

26. Bumper cars

27. Sandbars

28. Remembering what "calm" means

29. A good far cast

30. A black bikini

31. A nap on the beach, waking up with towel-nub indentations on your cheek, a little drool on the towel, and a

vast feeling of restedness

32. Noxema

33. Digging a tunnel next to yours, then digging a connecting tunnel and having our fingers meet in that crumbling moment

34. The smooth path of a wake behind the boat

35. A faded beach towel

36. Sandpipers

37. Water towers

38. The cricket that comes into the house and sings

39. The Shell Shop

40. Toe rings

41. A pervasive gray day and how soft it feels

42. When the carnival comes to town

43. Pulling a chair down to the low tide mark and letting the little waves lap around your feet

44. The smell of bacon in the morning

45. Wrap-around porches

46. Thinking of how you will learn the names of sea birds one day...

47. "Sex wax" surfboard wax

48. Walking the dog at night along the back streets, the warm light of other people's houses, the bustly chatter and clink of other people's lives as they clean up after dinner, the lonely but lovely way it feel to be alone and outside of that walking by...

49. Beach plum jelly made by a neighbor from a tree in her back yard

50. The scent of a bayberry leaf crushed

51. White corn with a pat of butter, salt and ground pepper

52. Floating

53. Always keeping an eye out for washed up treasure but being content never to find any

54. When your kids bury your legs and tell you that you can't move

55. Giddiness

56. Sand crabs

57. Puka shell necklaces

58. Taking the first breath of salty air as you come over the bridge

59. Not being able to wait to start reading your book again

60. Wading through a sun warmed tidal pool

61. A bushel basket of peaches at the farmer's market

62. "Ship Bottom" as the name for a town

63. Tiki bars

64. Riding your bike through a deep puddle

65. The enchanted fairy tale scent of wild roses in the dunes

66. The house that made it through the Hurricane of '44 and the story of the woman who rode it out in her attic and how she went mad afterwards and how her ghost still haunts that attic room and how, they say, you can hear her calling on stormy nights when the wind is right.

67. A rusty bike with a basket on the handlebars for when you go to get milk and the newspaper

68. Sitting on the red swivel stool at the Old Pharmacy and ordering a root beer float

69. Infatuation

70. A little pool of water in your belly button

71. Sun streaks in your hair

72. Humidity burning off

73. A Labrador swimming out for a stick and paddling back smiling and snorting and slick with glee

74. "Can you put some lotion on my back?"

75. Getting up early to go for doughnuts at the bakery

76. A storm scuttling across the bay

77. Two horseshoe crabs (attached)

78. A man happily floating in a pink
plastic tube in the ocean

79. When you make the turn on your bike and the wind
is at your back all the way home

80. The smell of Coppertone

81. The places that don't change

82. Half-green tomatoes ripening in the sun on the kitchen window sill

83. A baby in a white floppy hat sleeping on his father's shoulder

84. All the cars stopping to let a family of ducks waddle across the boulevard

85. Skim boards

86. Sparklers

87. An American flag on a shade dappled porch

88. The huge droopy face of a sunflower

89. Dusk

90. The froth of the ocean in a nor'easter

91. The rising falling insect hum of the marsh
at night

92. The warm bowl of water infused with lemon
that you dip your fingers in after you finish
your lobster

93. A pair of shoes left on the dune fence

94. The smell of low tide

95. Skee ball

96. O bla di O bla da boo bop a looba hubba dubba summer flim flam

97. The sun shining on your face

98. Soft ice cream (chocolate and vanilla swirl)

99. When the wind shifts

100. Other people packing their cars when you don't have to leave

Woman on Vacation

woman on
white sand

woman under
tree

woman on
blow-up raft

woman out
to sea

navigating

At the beach, directions can only take me so far. I'm on a perfectly good road, suddenly everything turns to sand...then I'm out to sea. The world is liquid and uncertain. I have to feel for my footing and start moving in a different way just to stay afloat. I know that any road that is worth anything does this—takes me somewhere new. Still, I'm scared silly (they don't call it the present TENSE for nothing). I tell myself, "I'm growing, I'm changing. This is good." But it's more imperative than that: Float. Drift. Dog paddle. Do something!

And don't let me swim back and try to get on that same old road. It'll just take me to the same old place. Here is where I am. In the liquid world. Surrounded by horizon. There's water in my ears, and I'm alone. On the other hand, I could go anywhere. From here, the world is possible.

Explorers thought the world had an edge, and they could fall off if they went wrong. I think they were right. The world is full of edges and falls. That horizon could be a new world, or it could be a cliff. This is still true. I look around me. The horizon is a line drawn in the sky...a kind of dare....

I could take out my FEAR MAP and say, "I'm going back to shore where it's safe and dry and there's that great little restaurant with the spicy chowder..." There's always a lot of logic to the fear map. It's very good at arguing and it's very convincing! And, you know, it attacks my weakest points...that chowder bit, now that was a low blow. Unfair really. And honestly, there's a sinking feeling in my heart when I think about going backwards. Backwards??? I ask you, is it really worth it, even considering the chowder? Exactly.

Or, I can use the I CAN THINK MY WAY OUT OF THIS MAP. But honestly, my brain has gotten me more lost than anything else in life. It thinks too much and chimes in with second guesses and distracting-other-options and let's-make-a-list detours and are-we-really-ready-yet doubts when I am just trying to GO somewhere and DO something. To my brain, I say, "Get in the back seat!" I give it a lot of crossword puzzles to do

so it stays busy, and it doesn't get in my way.

I could take out the STRAIGHT LINE MAP, the rigid little, "I know exactly where I am going and I'm not stopping anywhere..." map. Maybe I can convince myself of this if I say it with an even and intelligent voice, if I keep both hands on the wheel, if my hair-do doesn't become undone. The rigidity of this makes my neck hurt. Plus, my record at trying to control the world is downright pathetic. Isn't yours?

I could ask for help. Not such a bad idea. But, who to ask...? The guy with the GPS and the sleek zoomy car. There's something sure about him. He briskly turns corners, he maintains the crease in his pants. But does he get anywhere, does he ever figure out who he really is? I know there are other people like me. These are the people at rest stops forever unfolding maps, ignoring perfectly good directions and taking by-ways into recklessness, loop-de-looping for the giddy way it makes them feel, getting lost for the sheer befuddling trueness of the feeling. These are the people I understand. These are the people I trust. When I'm lost myself, these are the people I ask for directions. But they can't really tell me anything, and they know it.

Because it's my road. The wisest of them will tell me a good story and send me on my way. They know that the destination I have in mind is not what matters, that I may never get there, and that may be the best thing for me. The road is the only thing I have, and the only thing that counts is to get back on it...detours and traffic jams, beautiful scenery and stops along the way, stories and dead ends, swerves and accidents, and smooth smooth sailing. It's all going to happen. I'm just feeling my way. There's no such thing as directions.

So here I am on my own: Woman Without Map. Look at me now veering this way and that, willy-nilly-ing along... I get too easily distracted (as they told me in school). I have too much play in my steering wheel. Here I am treading water, looking at the sky. "This way, no, this way..." My heart and my body in their own happy argument. My brain interrupting incessantly. Sometimes they are ALL wrong. My body especially. But then again, it is so sweetly wrong, such a nice blend of soft and hard, smooth and rough, it dances and sings, gets goosebumpy at the thrilling parts, gets mushy at the lovely parts, walks me in good directions, pushes me into trouble, cries at all the awkward times, laughs me through disaster. Who can deny it?

I'll just set off. I'll use what I have. This crazy little body, this heart that goes on and on. This back seat brain. No external tools can help me. Who can navigate by stars? Who can follow a compass? What IS a sextant? This is all I know about navigation: A life is an engine meant for revving. Don't leave it in a dark corner idling. Give it interesting places to explore, let it dance with good partners, feed it on risk and winding adventure. Give it a comforting shoulder to lean on. Let it beat its own little drum.

I keep telling myself: Breathe. Taste. Smell. Feel. See. Hear. It seems so simple. But it is hard, very hard to keep doing this and keep doing it every moment. I keep forgetting. The air tries to remind me. The waves pound it at me, each one a different ride, a different possibility of floating or diving, drifting or swimming. The world keeps insisting itself like a lover. It says, "We'll never get this chance again, at this day, this moment, this right now. Take it. Take me. This is our time." I know...I know...

Navigation is this simple and this muddling: I am ALIVE, ALIVE, ALIVE! I hold the road in my arms. It's in my eyes and my hair. I am immersed in it. The road is not so much a place, a path, a plan, a WHERE. It's who I am. That's all I've really got. As Popeye says, "I Yam what I Yam..." That's where I'm going. That's how I'm getting there. That's my road.

how hard it is to catch the moment

too fast fish

too. much going on

hair blew in my eyes

incorrect Tool

blurry-- "you moved!"

well, after this I have to go to the grocery store, and let's see, what do I need, and then

thinking Too much

big blowfish belly in the way

oh, was I asleep?

wait... I wasn't ready

but I'm BUSY with REAL! and IMPORTANT things

Too filled with myself

change

Some days, dawn arrives like a good guest. It announces its approach shyly, gently, moving pinkly and sweetly into its place in the sky. It is on time, polite. The day is predictable. The guest bedroom is ready with fresh sheets, the refrigerator stocked, the whole house clean and ready.

But some days crack open. And you know that Change is here. Dawn is a hot gash in the sky. It's orange and red and purple. It's on fire and scary. The day is off and running wildly. Don't bother trying to catch your breath. Events snap open and shut, doors bang wide in a gust of wind, a storm blows up out of nowhere. Change is standing at the front door dripping in the rain: Take its coat. It's here for dinner. Set an

open the windows
Let it blow

extra place. Don't bother saying you're not ready. Wear whatever you're wearing. Pass the peas. Might as well light the candles and make the best of it.

Change is rude. It butts into conversations. It interrupts your train of thought, my sense of direction, the flow of the evening. Change keeps blurting directions: "Turn your heart on a dime. Accelerate. Skid. Do wheelies."

"Huh?" my brother is suddenly paying attention. He wants to know how to do a wheelie with your heart.

"Get lost," Change says.

"What?" I ask politely.

"Lost. Lost. Lost." Change says impatiently. "Get lost. Turn here. Let's go somewhere new."

I try to ask another question, but Change ignores me. Ignores us all. This isn't a conversation it is having. It just says what it feels, eats too much, burps repeatedly.

"Any cookies?" Change wants to know.

We're all still eating our main course. We look at our mother to see how she'll react. "Sweetness always helps," Change says. But it doesn't really care how we respond. It's already off on another tack. "Open all the windows, let it blow," Change says.

There's a storm crashing outside. The wind is slashing at the windows. Change is raising them up. The room is swirling with wind; the curtains are swooping like soggy ghosts; the candles are twisting and running in uneven rivulets. "Isn't this grand," Change says to no one in particular, whooshing around the table. "Isn't this wicked?"

It's so hard to have Change around. None of us wants Change to sit down next to him. But Change wants to trade seats with everyone, and we have to keep getting up and moving around. We're exhausted. We're not used to this. We can't wait for Change to leave.

"Shake it up," it keeps saying and laughing.

After dessert, we're looking toward the door making a kind of pathway with our eyes.

Change on the couch with grandma's afghan

But Change wants to sleep over. My mother is good with Change. She makes it a bed on the couch, fluffs up its pillow, gives it grandma's afghan. She stays up late talking to it like an old friend. We don't understand it at all. "How can she stand it?" I ask my brother. He shrugs.

When I wake up in the morning, Change is gone. There's a dent in the red couch and the afghan is tossed over one arm. There are puddles on the floor where the rain came in all night. My mother is on her knees wiping them up.

is Change coming back?

"Why isn't Change doing that?" I ask indignantly. I don't like to see my mother on her knees. She just laughs. "Change doesn't clean up after itself." I get down on my knees to join her.

Then we walk out on the porch to look at the waves. "Where did Change go?" I ask her. "Out," she says looking toward the water. We stand there a while looking at the waves rolling in, the pause of each wave, the fall, the frothy jumbly mess of its forward motion. The ocean is chaotic and vast and has that empty scary metallic look today. But it's beautiful too, thrilling really. I can feel the spray on my face. My mother smiles at me, "sweet," she says. I don't know if she's talking about Change or me or the ocean. All of us maybe.

"Is Change coming back?" I ask. Although I know already. Change hasn't really left. And it will never really leave. It's part of our family. Although it will always look like a stranger to us when it comes to the door.

I stand there with my mother feeling scared and excited and grown up. We are looking as far as the horizon...trying to take it all in.

storm

I love storms. I love storms with you. I love to open the sun roof and spread my arms to all the soaking rain while you drive. I love to stand on a high deck and be swirled by high winds and huddle against your chest. I love to unfold, and unloosen in all that wild air. I love to come undone with you.

And I love to race down the winding steps, following your shoulders, race you to the beach. I love to bend against a gust of wind and tuck into your shoulder. I love to hold your hand and feel like a kite reeling out into the far reach of the sky and then feel you pulling me back in. I love the frothy mixed up sea. We can't stay on the edge, because the edge keeps changing and surprising us and shoving us and pushing us and moving us. We are wetter than we planned. Roll up your pants. I love the sand slashing against my legs, against your legs, imbedding itself in us. Saying... Remember me. Remember me. I love how the lightning is following us and how we're running together trying to stay ahead of the storm. I love how we know we're going to get caught.

Look: I love the peony filled with rain. I love the tree blown of its leaves. The grasses leaning. I love how the marsh floods, all that was solid ground going under so quickly. How the salt meadow is a lake now. I love how a phantom boat floats up and moors itself here. The ring and rattle of its torn lines. Will it leave in the next storm? I love the grey black fluid endless sky, how it flies all around us. How it makes us believe we could fly too, if, oh something..., maybe we just spread our arms out wider or leaned out a little further. Something that feels so close to what we have, what we are.

Let's put on clean warm clothes and go for a drive in it. Let it slash and patter the car, let it blind us and bury the main road. Put on the thin little wiper blades as fast as they can go. Clickclickclickclick. Down the road is nothing but blur, maybe the world has lost its friction. We are sliding into blue into gray into pure mood. Pause us here, in this bar with the light in the window, with the dusk darker than it should be. I love the mist blowing against the windows. I love the world knee deep in puddles. Take your shoes off and run.

We're drenched with emotion. The little hairs on your arm are standing up. I love the glowy dim lights in this bar, the lonely beery smell, the Yankee game going on the TV in the corner, "Band of Gold" playing on the juke box. I love the smooth round edge of the bar. The bartender is betting on Johnny Be Good in the third race. We are watching all the TV's at once. We are drinking something that burns. We know this much: The Yankees are winning, then they are losing. All the talk is about gambling. All the outcomes are unknown. We wish for right now: Let the storm continue. Let it keep us here longer.

I love the mood streaking across your face, the cloud in your eye. I love the sound of the rain slashing against that window. I am watching your mind, and can see each page turning in your heart, how your glasses sit quietly on the bridge of your nose and how you glance at me over them. I love how all the weather in the world is in that moment.

No predictions can help us. You be the thunder and I'll be the lightning. You be the wind and I'll be the rain. Right now: This is our storm.

La Luna

moonLiT LaUndry

moon
doggie

La Luna, La Luna
mother Moon

moon dance

the moon is sorry

I grew up in a family of beach women: My mother and her sisters and cousins and friends. As for fathers and husbands? They were only weekenders in the summer. For all the other days, for the entire basking glorious sunny summer, our house, and our beach, and really our whole childhood world was filled with beach women.

Here's to the days that they created! Glorious and carefree summers that were more idyllic than is possible... What they created was peace-stretching long yawning thrilling warm ease. Who ever saw them struggle? Each day unfolded without effort. They were there to take us to the beach or to the bay, pump up our rafts, help us build and bury, bait our hooks, untangle our lines, wrap us in warm towels after we were in the waves for hours and hours pickled and pruned and carry us home. Our beach house was swept clean and filled with sunshine, stocked with cookies, steaming with white corn, sizzling with flounder in a pan of browned butter. Anyone could eat over. Everyone was welcome. The shelves were stacked with well worn chapter books and crossword puzzles, books of mazes and elaborate coloring books alongside a mug of sharp colored pencils, a box of playing cards and a box of pinochle cards. And nobody ever seemed to be too tired or too busy to play.

Now a mother myself, I have nothing of their endless uncomplaining energy. I wonder at it. I never noticed them struggling (maybe because childhood is about not noticing). I wonder if their husbands were not really noticing either (those were different times). I think of those summers and I wonder when they had a chance to be women — to be something other than care-givers. Were they too tired to even look for the chance?

Here's to their sacrifice so willingly given. Here's to the summers they made. Here's to the nursery rhyme day off they should have taken — luscious and selfish enough to make even the moon sorry. I wish I had seen them this way...

My old Ma and My Aunt Dolly
sky green eyes and laughter jolly
folding chaise and pop-a-lolly
hush a bye surf and wind no squally
gone to the beach flim flam folly
won't come back till the moon is sorry
won't come back till the moon is sorry

Nap all day and popsically
dreamy dream and no no guilty
undone hair and sun dress freely
tilt and whirl and laughter dreamy
gone far far from reality
won't come back till the moon is sorry
won't come back till the moon is sorry

Dance your step by the whale tail belly
moon so shine and jellyfish jelly
night so dark and star shine fell-y
wildness howl and your story telly
life is short and love is call-y
don't come back till the moon is sorry
don't come back till the moon is sorry

Wadey and shadey, paradey ladies
dive your dive in the dippity day

don't come back till the sun is fadey
don't come back till the grass is hay
don't come back till the kids are sleepy
don't come back till the dads are frayed
don't come back till the moon is sorry
don't come back all sunny day
don't come back till the moon is sorry
don't come back till you've done your day

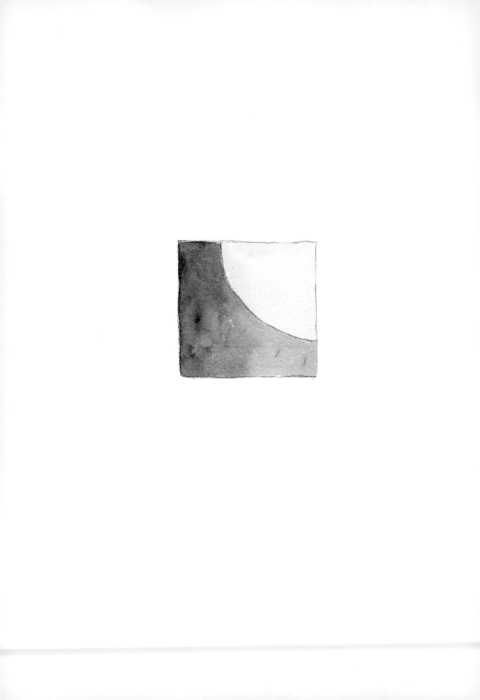

Beach Woman-y Rhyme

hey diddle diddle,
Sometimes Life
makes me feel Little,

I want To jump
over the moon.

My fat dog Laughs
To see such fun,

And my stove ran away
with my vacuum.

Hey diddle diddle,
I'm a beach woman
aged (middLe),

Let me sing
a Laziness Tune.

Let my dog dance
with me in the crazy Sun,

Let midnight faLL
in Love with noon.

outside shower

There's a tinge of rust in the air, a hint of mildew, an old-board wet sand smell. A cobweb droops in the corner. The cap to an ancient shampoo bottle is wedged in the floorboards. No one will ever get it out. No one will ever try.

The soap has been here a while in this enamel soap dish that Kevin screwed to the wall a little crookedly. There's a layer of sand embedded in it. And that one shampoo that nobody likes has been here for 2 years. It sits on the wooden ledge with Karyl's rusty barrette and the perfect little black scallop shell. It doesn't change much in here. The door rattles a bit when the breeze blows. But time can't get in. It's always August in here, always the luscious middle of vacation. Reality is always a good month away...This is the place where summer stays. See, there's the 1996 Surf Fishing

Tournament hat hanging on the hook, there's the faded towel a little stiff with salt, there's the bathing suit dripping.

In this secret gloomy little half-room, I'm removed from the world But I'm only 50 feet away from my neighbor's deck where he is barbecuing. "Hon," he calls to his wife, "can you bring me the spatula?" The screen door slaps. I can hear another outside shower running too–down the street. I slide my bathing suit off and make it into a sodden pile with my feet. The shower is streaming all over me its slow irregular rainy beat, its lukewarm softness. I am utterly naked. I am rivulets. I am pelted with ease. I am washed and un-salted. I am freshened-up. The air is swirling around my legs. I smell hamburgers sizzling on the barbecue. Someone else's kid yells, "Mom?" I am soaping up and frothy. My skin is squeaking. Why are tan lines so sweet and interesting and appealing? Inside the house, my family is bustling around without me, or perhaps just lazily thinking about dinner. This is contentment. I am in a stall of rain; I am my own box of weather. This must be what a cloud feels like when it comes home from its long flight, but nobody knows it's home yet. It's just standing on the doorstep feeling the nearness of being there. Feeling light, homey, arrived but not yet burdened with arrival.

I am a mermaid. I am fishy and wild, domestic and exotic. This is as mundane as standing under a faucet, but I feel like something primal, an out-island woman. A waterfall, a sky. This is a church of the outside kind. I am washed of my mind. I am washed of the past and the future. It's all present in here. It's all pause. The strawberry cheap shampoo, the grit of the soap, the jar of lead sinkers that nobody knows how to dispose of on the shelf. "Yoohoo," someone calls from next door. It's not for me. This is heaven, I tell you, this is heaven.

beach hats

Leave crabby behind

anything that my grandchildren give me, I glue on this hat.

viable alternative energy source

no sunburned ears

the Skipper

beach badge chic

haute couture: watch out for wind gusts

radical wave
dude

no, that's a frisbee

imperfect and frayed but very fine: wear with pride

howdy

vast and mysterious also serves as a beach umbrella

and they
lived
happily
ever after

Once upon a time, there was a beach ♀ . The beach ♀ loved the ~~~. She loved the smell of it, the peace of it, the cool of it. She had loved it since she was a young 👤. Now she was grown with three 👥👥👥 of her own. Today, the ☀ was shining and there was not a ☁ in the sky. The 👥👥👥 wanted to go to the ~~~. So the beach ♀ gathered up their stuff and off they went. She was carrying a big 🛍 with peanut butter and jelly 🍞 s for everyone, and one catsup 🍞 for Johnny because that's all he ate. She was carrying J U I C E for all, a big bag of chips , beach 🌀 and SPF 15 .

She was carrying a huge beach , and many s and s.

You could almost not see her, she was carrying so many things. She felt like

a in the desert.

She teetered and tottered her way up to the dune to the .

She found a spot and arranged all of her belongings and unfolded her

It had a nice sling back and a comfy seat and wide arms and she knew that,

when she sank into it, she would feel like she could sink further and further

into the nice warm sand until only her was sticking out. The beach

woman needed a nap. Perhaps she always needed a .

But the kids wanted to go jump in the . So they jumped and

jumped till there was no jump left in their . And the

beach woman felt like a rubber . Then they wanted to go boogie

ing. So they boogied and boogied till there was no boogie left in

their hearts. The beach woman was as sodden as a . Then little

Johnny was hungry for his catsup but he dropped it in the

and cried and cried until there were no  left in his .

It was at times like this that the beach felt pulled in so many different

directions that she felt like an with eight arms.

She sat down on the . Little Johnny started to bury her. So

she helped him mound up the sand until it covered her . The rest

of the joined in, and they covered her and her

up to her neck. They decorated her with s and shells

until she was covered from to and she looked like a big

. The beach felt peaceful for a moment. But just for one

moment. "See if you can break out!" Johnny said. So she did. She had sand

in her and her and her and even her . So

they all went into the to wash off.

By this time, the was low in the sky. The beach woman had

not yet sat in her lovely . Nor had she felt the shade of her

beautiful beach . Nor had she read one page of her .

It was time to go home.

All the kids got in the outside . Then the beach woman rinsed out

their s And wrapped them in warm s and fed them s

with .While they ate, the beach sighed and collapsed in a

heap on the She felt like a jelly with all the goop

sucked out of it, flattened and sunbaked and dried out. The children ate in

one minute. Then they gathered around her and asked her if she could read

them the about the witch in a castle. She looked at them like a

growly . She was so grimy and grumpy and hugely sleepy that

she felt like she could eat all of her children or (if not that) go to

and hibernate for three months. But instead, the beach woman put her witch

on her head, and Johnny gave her the big barbecue

to be her wand, and she read them the whole wicked .

Three times.

When her husband came home, he found the beach 👤 still on the couch, still un-showered and in her 👙 , with a sunburned 👃 , and her witch 🎩 askew. He stood and looked at her and his 👀 s got all 💧💧💧 -y. And his 👄 broke into a ⌣ . He said, "You are so beautiful.". And the beach 👤 felt not like a 🐫 , or a 🐢 , or a rubber 🎾 , or an 🐙 with eight legs, or a jelly 🐟 with all the goop sucked out of it, or even a growly 🐻 who wanted to eat her children. The beach woman felt like the ☀ was shining inside of her. She felt like she could do anything (even stay awake a little bit longer!).

The beach woman felt like a woman again.

still working
on herself

you and me in a house by the sea

Don't go to Sedona to look for a vortex. Or travel to Peru to find the spiritual center of the universe. It's right here where you put yourself. It's how you lay your towel down, where you stand that beach umbrella, how you aim your beach chair. And make room for me in that sunshine...

Here we are facing out to sea, each on our own chairs. You are digging little holes with your feet, then you are forming little walls. This is what you do. I put my foot on top of yours and you glance at me and smile. This is how we are together.

You want to read me something from your book. I want to watch your finger run over the edge of the page, hear the rumbling happy tone of your voice, hear the story in it and your desire to interest me. The way you inflect that word, and that one... Hear that? The way you want me to be in on it, that joke, that slant of vision. Then I know you want to go back to your own reading. It is so lovely to be so close and so separate. I love not to reach for you but just be aware of you next to me. I love to meet your eyes, look away.

You get up and go stand in the water. Your back looks strong and sinewy. You look distant and deep, like a philosopher at the edge of the world. Then you give out a whoop and gallumph into the waves like a gangly wild boy. I hear a final hoot and then you crash sideways into the foam of a wave. You pop out like a seal, carousing with yourself, toying with the waves, riding them and lollopping over them. I join after a while, in my own quieter way, and we ride some waves together, grinning at each other at the shoreline, our bathing suits askew, our hair unruly and plastered wrong-ways to our heads.

When we get out, we walk along the edge of the water. It's low tide. We don't say much. Still, when I show you that perfect little shell, you nod at me happily. When you bend, I know it will be to pick up that broken shell, a ragged sculpted old thing. You hold my hand for a time. When we turn back, you pull me close, hold me quietly. Then we walk back. "See the color of that sky," you ask. "Yup," I tell you.

If we were spiders, every word would carry a silver thread. Every glance, every gesture, every thing said and unsaid would be weaving us closer. There is a tangible energy in the world. It is not just in those canyons out west, or ancient spiritual burial grounds. It is right here. It is in you, and it is in me. We can feel ourselves like tuning forks emanating some high pitched sound that our ears can't hear, but still, it is raising the pitch of our hearts, it's making the hair rise on the back of your neck and sending some frisson of thrill right through me. We can feel it so intensely because we are in love. But we all have it. Each of us. Apart. Every person has his own tuning fork, his own invisible silver thread, his own energy that keeps emanating into the world touching and moving things. And the world is doing it back. We are all in invisible conversation with each other; we are all weaving the web of the world.

At the beach, this all seems clearer. Even when I am alone. Even when I am missing you and bereft, I am in love with the world, with the beach, with its gestures and whoops, the way its hair sticks out, the way it walks with me distant and then close. The way it tells me a story. The way it puts a chair down next to me. Oh world, we are together... make room for me in that sunshine...

Sunse T S

shy:
hid behind
cloud

Lingering:
can't say goodbye

fasT and sneaky:
too bad,
you looked away

mad! slam shut
no coLor
insTanT night

remember
how LiTTle
you are

kiss her
you fooL

field goaL:
three poinTs

Swish

I was abducTed
by a gianT energy
field that Took
over my head

shine: this is your moment

70

Sometimes I think
all I really need in Life
is in my beach bag.

About the Author

Sandy Gingras is an artist and writer with her own design company called "How To Live" (visit her website at www.how-to-live.com). She and her son and two cats live near the beach on an island in New Jersey, where she is active in efforts to preserve open space and wetlands.

If you liked this book, you'll also enjoy these other books by Sandy Gingras:

Reasons to be Happy at the Beach
ISBN 0-945582-98-6

"Happiness is all around us. We are looking at it, breathing it, holding it in our hands."

How to Live at the Beach
ISBN 0-945582-73-0

"Like the ocean itself, this book nourishes the mind, heart, and soul."
— Coastal Living Magazine

At the Beach House - A Guest Book
ISBN 1-59322-006-5

A great way to remember all your visitors with sandy feet.

How to Live on an Island
ISBN 0-945582-57-9

"...there's no truer place than an island."

The Uh-oh Heart
ISBN 0-945582-96-X

For all of us with uh-oh hearts fearful of growing and risking and loving.

How to be a Friend
ISBN 0-945582-99-4

A little book that celebrates friendship.

The annual
How to Live at the Beach:
Year-Round Calendar

Down The Shore Publishing offers other book and calendar titles (with a special emphasis on the coast). For a free catalog, or to be added to our mailing list, just send us a request.

Down The Shore Publishing
P.O. Box 3100 ❖ Harvey Cedars, NJ 08008
or email: info@down-the-shore.com
www.down-the-shore.com